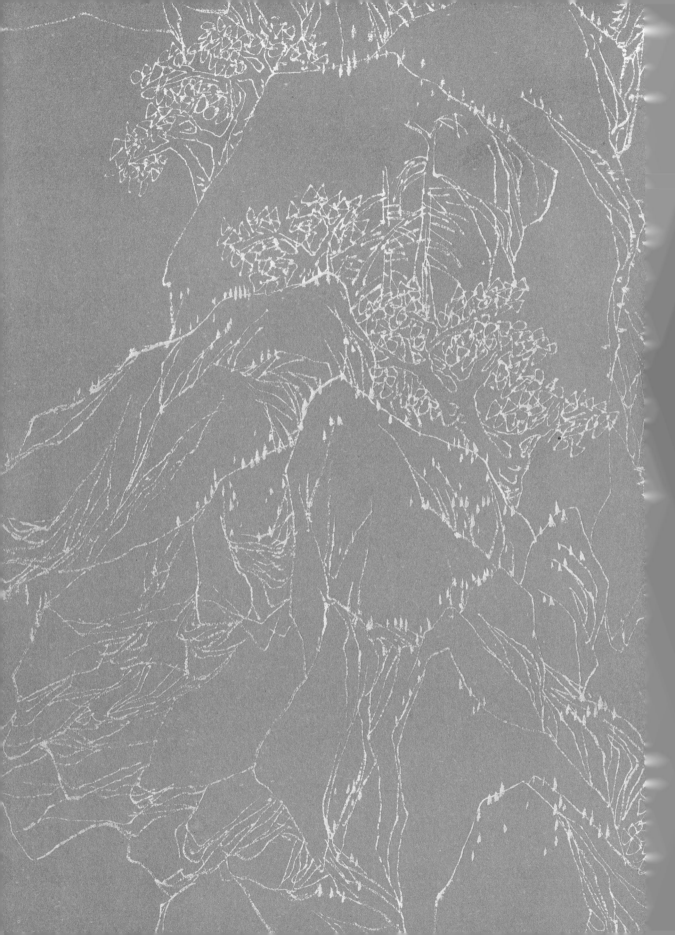

CELEBRATED CHINESE HISTORICAL FIGURES

Painted in traditional Chinese style by
Wang Xijing
and
Wang Mingming

With biographical notes compiled by
Ma Yue
and
Wang Yanrong

Morning Glory Publishers
Beijing 1989

Calligraphy of book title in Chinese: Jiang Zhaohe
Cover picture: Lin Yong

First edition 1989

Publisher:
Morning Glory Publishers
(A subsidiary of China International Book Trading Corporation)
Chegongzhuang Xilu 21, Beijing, China

Distributor:
China International Book Trading Corporation (Guoji Shudian)
P.O. Box 399, Beijing, China

Printed in the People's Republic of China

Images from History

(An Introduction)
by Cai Ruohong

The figures depicted in this book are persons renowned in Chinese history for their talents, deeds and contributions to their fellow men. They left behind their works — brilliant feats, legends and written records, but no portraits of them existed until artists Wang Xijing and Wang Mingming decided to "create" them. To aid their creation, these contemporary artists consulted literary accounts and all available materials, but declined to use any visible images as models. Thus the present "portraits" are the crystallization of the reasoning, imagination and artistry of the painters.

China possesses a time-honored tradition in the painting, sculpture and carving of historical figures. The Unicorn Pavilion of the Han Dynasty (206 BC-220 AD) and the Rising Mist Pavilion of the Tang (618-907) were both built more than a thousand years ago, at the order of emperors, to house portraits of heroes as a means of honoring them. Unfortunately, those paintings have been lost with the passage of time. Occasionally one can find statues of historical persons among those of the Buddhas, emperors and nobles enshrined in ancient Chinese temples, caves or tombs. These, however, were often idealized, not realistic, so that the faces and bodies look almost identical, and very few of them remain intact today. Other images of historical figures, painted or carved, can be seen in ancient books and paintings and on stone tablets, but again, few are found in these sources. Thus many outstanding persons of ancient China do not occupy the place they deserve in the plastic arts, and it is the duty of modern artists to bridge this gap.

The creation of images of historical figures based on research and imagination emerged as interest in them grew, and has now become a special branch of art for modern painters and sculptors. In the thirty-nine years since the founding of new China, more and more paintings and sculptures of this kind have appeared. Museums, memorial halls, parks, squares, books and pictorial journals display them to encourage patriotism and enthusiasm for history, and to foster a desire to learn from the heroes of ancient China. Art can produce unexpectedly good effects when it reaches the masses of people.

Wang Xijing and Wang Mingming, both middle-aged artists, have been painting for half their lives. Each has his own unique style: Mingming paints in a bold, vigorous, almost exaggerated way, while Xijing creates elegant and graceful figures. Both employ the techniques of traditional Chinese figure painting, but modify them to meet the aesthetic requirements of modern times.

Here it may be pertinent to deal briefly with the method of creating portraits of historical figures. The essential guidelines are these:

1. Do not proceed from mere imagination, but study carefully all available written materials about the hero's life and deeds. Then deliberate and form an idea about the subject's temperament, whether bold, uninhibited, optimistic, devoted, timid or melancholy. Begin painting the hero's face and body only when you have a clear conception of his temperament. Images of historical figures, however well they are painted, do not appeal to the viewer if they come purely from the artist's imagination. Artistic response arises only when the image coincides largely with that formed by the viewer through his reading. Knowledgeable viewers, like artists, have their own imaginatin, which comes from the same source — written materials. Therefore, the artist must read extensively in order to create successful portraits.

2. Depict the figure in an appropriate activity, the best way to show

his temperament. Bodhidharma (?-528 or 536), who sat motionless facing a wall for nine years, is an exception, but this very inactivity characterizes him. Certainly, the key to capturing a person's spirit is to paint the action that most vividly reflects his character, demeanor, interest and emotion. Ancient Chinese masters of figure painting set good examples for this in their works. Their characters, even fictitious ones, are vivid and lifelike as depicted in action.

3. The arrangement of background is a matter closely related to the vivid presentation of a figure. Ancient masters of figure painting always regarded background as important in revealing the personality of their subject. The background, whether an indoor scene or outdoor landscape, should contain appropriate objects representing the life or characteristics of the figure. Traditionally, we are familiar with some well-known personages and their accompanying symbols: Tao Yuanming with a chrysanthemum, Su Wu with sheep, Zheng Banqiao with bamboo, Lin Heqing with plums, Qu Yuan with water, Wang Xizhi with a goose, Zhong Kui with a sword, and Mi Dianzhi with stones. These visual clues do not require a lot of brushwork, only slight indications, because they are familiar motifs.

The appearance of the figures, whether tall, short, handsome or ugly, is a secondary matter and the artist can depict as he sees fit. The general viewer will accept the artist's rendering. Different painters may depict the same figure in various ways, reflecting their particular source materials, personal interpretation, and means of expression. What the viewer appreciates is the resemblance to the spirit of the subject, not a formal likeness.

Qi Baishi (1863-1957), the great master of Chinese painting, once said that a balance must be struck between "likeness" and "unlikeness" in painting a portrait. What he implied is that the temperament of a subject must be accurately portrayed, although his appearance and movement may not be exact. And, for greater impact, the demeanor of the hero must be exaggerated, while elements which are not essential in displaying character must be deleted. There can be no exaggeration without deletion. The two both oppose and complement each other. The works of Wang Xijing and Wang Mingming exemplify Qi Baishi's theory.

Dissimilar cultures and ways of perception make understanding Chinese art difficult for some Western scholars. I am confident, however, that this gap will shrink and eventually disappear through frequent exposure to China's art, and that books such as this one will no doubt contribute to greater understanding.

Celebrated Chinese Historical Figures

KONG QIU

Kong Qiu (551-479 B.C.), styled Zhongni, is better known in the West as Confucius.

Confucius' forefathers were nobles of the state of Song at a time when China was divided into many small states. His great grandfather moved to the state of Lu when his political career failed. Confucius' father became a secretary in Zou County (present-day Qufu in Shandong Province). When Confucius was born, his family's position had already declined.

As a boy, Confucius worked in a warehouse and tended cows and sheep. He also worked as a helper to a master of funeral ceremonies for the nobles. Recalling his childhood he later said, "I was poor and lowly when young. That's why I can do humble things." Like many other children of ruined families, he often recalled the glory and wealth of the past. But Confucius had an old head upon his young shoulders. He was serious and thoughtful whether he was playing or attending a funeral. When he became a young man, he grew interested in the decrees and regulations of the Western Zhou Dynasty, called the Zhou Rites, which he later annotated and spread.

Many social reforms and differing ideologies emerged in China during Confucius' time. Rationalism displaced primitive sorcery and religious and traditional ideas, laying the foundation for the development of Chinese culture.

Confucian philosophy played a very important role in creating Chinese culture and psychology. Confucius used rationalist ideas to re-explain primitive culture. He applied the principles of ritual to daily life, emotions and political concepts. He promoted behavioural standards combined with benevolence.

Confucius' life-long motto was, "Be insatiable in learning and teaching." With "3,000 disciples and 70 worthies," he was a famous educator in his time. He forwarded theories on politics, ethics, music, education, and funeral and wedding ceremonies. He lectured much, but left behind only one written work, *Lun Yu* (*The Analects of Confucius*), which was compiled by his disciples. He also revised *Shi Jing* (*The Book of Songs*), the first collection of songs and poems in China, and during his later years worked on the history book *Chun Qiu* (*The Spring and Autumn Annals*).

Wang Mingming:
Kong Qiu

LAO ZI

Lao Zi (580-500 B.C.), also called Lao Dan, was a historian-official of the state of Chu.

Lao Zi was aloof, but he professed a deep understanding of life and the universe. He was as great a thinker as Confucius, but Lao Zi dismissed the notion that taking a positive attitude towards politics was the way to bring order to the world. Instead, he believed a country would achieve stability only through noninterference. He described the relationship between a ruler and his subjects this way, "I govern by doing nothing and the people will be civilized; I keep silent and the people will be honest; I remain idle and the people will get rich; I reject desire and the people will be simple."

Believing that all social conflict was rooted in desire, Lao Zi condemned petty fighting and internal struggles. Living in a time when dukes were constantly vying with each other, Lao Zi longed for the primitive way of life when people lived in harmonious communities.

In his work *Lao Zi*, Lao Zi named "dao" as the source of all life and the shapeless order of things, which a human being cannot actually observe. He said, "Like the Emperor, I don't know who is whose son." Lao Zi's "dao," as a philosophical concept, was later understood as something absolute. Out of it grew *xuanxue*, a philosophical sect during the Wei (220-265) and Jin (265-420) dynasties.

Wang Mingming:
Lao Zi

QU YUAN

China's earliest and greatest poet, Qu Yuan (340?-278? B.C.) was actually named Qu Ping. A noble of the state of Chu during the Warring States Period, Qu Yuan was a well-educated, astute statesman. In his 20s he held a high position in the court of Emperor Huai of Chu, "discussing state affairs with the emperor before he issued orders and meeting guests to cope with the dukes."

Later he clashed with the corrupt officials in the court over how to deal with the state of Qin, the most powerful state at that time. He stood for an alliance with the state of Qi to oppose Qin. But his idea was opposed in the court, and he was twice exiled to the southern Yangtze River area.

While Qu Yuan was in exile, the state of Chu was gradually swallowed up by Qin. Finally, when Qu Yuan was in his 60s, he threw himself into a river, drowning his sorrows with him.

Qu Yuan left behind many poems, including *Lisao, Tianwen, Zhaohun, Huaisa and Simeiren*. Interweaving his rich imagination and deep emotions, these poems describe the melancholy which hung over Qu Yuan's mind like a dark cloud and his loyalty and devotion to his homeland.

Lisao, Qu Yuan's most brilliant poem, is representative of his work in exile. With 373 lines, it is the longest ancient Chinese poem. It depicts the pain of a pure and loyal man suffering from solitude, suppression, melancholy and despair. Sometimes he tells himself to wait for exoneration from the emperor and sometimes he loses his patience and sighs at the blue sky.

Deep in his heart, he yearns for a bright future. "The emperor came to Beizhu, worry in his eyes; Autumn wind blows, Dongtin Lake ripples and tree leaves fall."

In his public life, Qu Yuan was an outstanding representative of feudal officialdom. But his poems made him a pioneer of romanticism in Chinese literature.

Wang Xijing:
Qu Yuan

QIN SHIHUANG

Born during the Warring States Period, Emperor Qin Shihuang (259-210 B.C.) was an outstanding Chinese statesman.

Beginning life as an ordinary Qin prince named Ying Zhen, he came to the throne when he was 13, and officially began his reign at 21.

During the Warring States Period, China was marked by social change. Dukes enlarged their armies and set up separate regimes. They put up barricades, built city walls and fought each other. Finally the land was ruled by seven rival principalities: Chu, Qi, Yan, Han, Zhao, Wei and Qin. Qin was the most powerful.

When Qin Shihuang came to power, he adopted the suggestion of his advisor Li Si: "Fight to become emperor by eliminating all the other principalities and unifying China." Qin Shihuang spent 10 years destroying the other principalities and finally founded the Qin Dynasty in 221 B.C. It was the first unified, centralized feudal society in China, and Qin Shihuang named himself emperor.

Qin Shihuang proved to be a wise, decisive emperor and an excellent military strategist. He oversaw all major political matters himself. He organized the unified country into 36 prefectures divided into counties, and directly appointed all the important officials at the central and local levels.

Qin Shihuang instituted a series of political, economic and cultural reforms. He unified the national laws, measures, money and written language. He also revised the calendar and repaired many roads. Representing the new landlord class, Qin Shihuang ruthlessly opposed the restoration of slavery in Qin.

For protection from the Xiongnu (Hun) to the north, Qin Shihuang ordered the sections of the Great Wall built by various dukes to be connected. The 5,000-km-long wall, symbolizing the nation's strong will, is the pride of the Chinese even today. He also built the grandiose Epang Palace and tombs for himself on Li Mountain.

Much money and millions of people were involved in these projects, which required heavy corvée, rent and taxes, and cruel pressed labour. The people suffered a great deal. One year after Qin Shihuang's death in 209 B.C., the peasants revolted for the first time in Chinese history. After two years of bloody war, the Qin Dynasty was toppled. But Qin Shihuang's feudal system remained.

Wang Mingming:
Qin Shihuang

秦始皇造像
歲在己年秋月
明□書

Xiang Yu and Liu Bang were leaders of two insurgent armies. They joined the forces of King Huai of Chu to fight the main Qin army. When the fall of the Qin Dynasty was doubtless, they fought each other for power. The struggle lasted four years, from 205 to 202 B.C., and is known in Chinese history as the War Between the Chu and the Han.

XIANG YU

Xiang Yu (232-202 B.C.) was a native of Xiaxiang in present-day Jiangsu Province. His grandfather, Chu general Xiang Yang, fought fiercely with the Qin army, but committed suicide after defeat. At that time Xiang Yu was 10 years old. When he was 11, the Qin defeated the Chu and the other five principalities and unified China (221 B.C.).

Xiang Yu was very stubborn, even as a child. He did not like to read. When he had trouble developing his swordplay techniques, he read a few books on military tactics and strategy.

One day Xiang Yu saw the procession of Emperor Qin Shihuang. Seeing the emperor's majesty, the boy said to his uncle, "I can replace him!"

In 207 B.C. Xiang Yu, then 25, killed the leader of the anti-Qin insurgent troops he had joined and took over the top position. He was a brave fighter and general. In 208 B.C. he led his 20,000 soldiers against the Qin army at Julu. When they had crossed the Zhangshui River (a branch of the Yellow River), he ordered all the boats sunk and told each man to carry food for only three days, expressing his confidence of victory. As a result, his men defeated a Qin army of 200,000, laying a solid foundation for a complete rebel victory.

Xiang Yu then led 400,000 soldiers into Xianyang, where they burned down the Qin palaces. He established his capital in Pengchen in 206 B.C. and called himself the "Hegemonic King of Western Chu". But he had no real interest in ruling the country. He merely wished to dominate all the other dukes. Due to his cruelty, more and more dukes turned their loyalty to his rival Liu Bang.

In the winter of 202 B.C. Xiang Yu's troops arrived in what is now Linbi County in Anhui Province, where they were besieged by Liu Bang's troops. One night Liu Bang's soldiers sang songs from Chu, making Xiang Yu's men homesick. Xiang Yu, terribly upset, walked through the camp drinking with his beautiful concubine, Yuji. Feeling uneasy, Xiang Yu recalled his military life and sang:

For lifting a mountain I've no match in the world;
Plagued by a luck so bad that my horse refuses to gallop.
What can I do with the horse refusing to move?
Alas, Yu, what can I do for you?"

In tears, Yuji sang together with Xiang Yu. Then sinking into despair, she used his sword to cut her throat.

Xiang Yu led his troops to fight their way out. When they reached the Wujiang River, he had only a few followers left. Xiang Yu killed himself with his sword.

Wang Mingming:
Xiang Yu

LIU BANG

Liu Bang (256-195 B.C.), also called Ji, was a native of Peixian County in present-day Jiangsu Province. Born into a middle-class peasant family, Liu Bang knew much about the peasants. He also had a small official post and, because of this, he knew the landlords just as well. Liu Bang overcame his rival, Xiang Yu, because of this knowledge.

Liu Bang also had a broad mind. When Xiang Yu proclaimed himself king, he offered Liu Bang an official post as King of the Han, with a capital in Nanzhen (present-day Nanzhen County in Shaanxi). At the time, Liu Bang was militarily weaker than his rival.

Once, Xiang Yu's advisor, Fang Zhen, suggested to kill Liu Bang. Xiang Yu deployed 400,000 troops at Hongmen and invited Liu Bang to attend a banquet there. Liu Bang knew about the plot and flattered Xiang Yu to survive the banquet. Later, when the dukes turned their backs against Xiang Yu, Liu Bang took advantage and fought Xiang Yu for power. By making a series of tactically clever manoeuvres, using defense as offense and relying on a strong rear guard for support, Liu Bang finally triumphed despite repeated losses.

In 202 B.C.Liu Bang became emperor,a representative of the newly emerging landlord class. He began the Western Han Dynasty, which lasted until 24 A.D.

Wang Xijing:
Liu Bang

大風起兮雲飛揚，威加海內兮歸故鄉，安得猛士兮守四方。漢高祖劉邦平定黥布叛亂後，率軍途經家鄉沛縣，置酒宴歡，歌於喜之情自心詠出，這就是有名的高祖歌，並撃筑於沛宮。當其即席起舞，隨聲高歌，辛巳年夏於西京　王□寫大風歌

□

SIMA XIANGRU

Also known as Changqing, Sima Xiangru (179-117 B.C.) was a native of Chengdu in Sichuan Province. He was a well-known scholar during the Western Han Dynasty. When he was a young man he loved to read and practice swordplay. By chance Emperor Hanwu read his poetic work *Zixu Fu* and decided the author was a master of *fu*, a kind of prose-poem.

Sima Xiangru was very poor at the time, but very proud. Later he made friends with Zhuo Wangsun, a wealthy person in Sichuan, and fell in love with his daughter, Zhuo Wenjun. In the evenings he played the *qin*, a stringed instrument, to court Wenjun. Later they boldly eloped to Chengdu, where he opened a liquor store. "Wenjun listening to *qin* playing" has since been the subject of many poems and paintings showing the enchantment of love.

Sima Xiangru made a name for himself writing *fu* verse, which reached its apex during the Han Dynasty. By then it has grown from a very primitive dance drama into a literary art.

Fu works are often exaggerated. In *Zixu Fu* Sima Xiangru wrote, "In a dream I travel on clouds 900 *li*, seeing mountains..." His descriptions of landscapes in this work are quite fantastic. Like paintings from a dream, Sima Xiangru set his imagination free when writing *fu* verse. His writing captures the liveliness and the imaginative effect of music.

The incredible imagination shown in *fu* verse stemmed from the social life of the Han Dynasty, an extremely prosperous time for China after the Qin Dynasty. Han art covered every aspect of life, from ancestors to heroes to peasants, from immortals to chickens.

The *fu* Sima Xiangru wrote were so famous during his life that he was asked by an emperor's concubine, who had lost his favor, to write a *fu* to move the heart of the ruler.

Wang Xijing:
Sima Xiangru

司馬相如字長卿蜀郡成都人西漢辭賦家其代表作一座賦為武帝光賞因得召見又作上林賦武帝周悅師十蜀中賢士結為司馬文園集卿由舞王西京造

WANG ZHAOJUN

Wang Zhaojun, also called Qiang, was a palace maid of Emperor Yuandi of the Western Han Dynasty in the middle of the first century B.C. She was born in Jiegui (now Jiegui County in Hubei Province), and is remembered for marrying a man of the Xiongnu nationality to cement friendly ties between the Han and the Xiongnu peoples.

An ancient nomadic tribe, the Xiongnu became powerful in the third century B.C. and declined in the first century A.D. The tribe was very active for about 300 years during the Han Dynasty. Later it continued activities for another 200 years in the Central Plains, exerting a great influence on Chinese history.

In the early years of the Han Dynasty, China was weak. To maintain peace in the border area, the emperor sent many valuable gifts to the Xiongnu, including cotton, liquor, gold and silk. Brides were also sent in 198 B.C., but this failed to stop the border harrassment.

Emperor Wudi waged two decisive wars against the Xiongnu in the north, beginning in 133 B.C. The tribe was decimated.

In 33 B.C. Wang Zhaojun was sent to the Xiongnu as a gesture of friendship from the Han Dynasty to its enemy. Huhanxie, leader of the Xiongnu, was so grateful that he promised to be a friend of the Hans.

According to historical records, Wang Zhaojun volunteered to marry a Xiongnu. At the farewell banquet she was sweet. graceful and beautiful.

Wang Zhaojun was not the first or the last aristocratic woman sent to the Xiongnu as a bride. But she is remembered because she was perhaps the only one who went "willingly". Some say she did it out of patriotism. Others say she had been out of favor with the emperor for many years, and made the sacrifice with great resentment. When she left, the emperor felt deep pity for her.

Scholars through the years have tried to understand Wang Zhaojun's motivations. They believe that her poignant love for the emperor and the Han people was mixed with a dislike of the emperor's attitude towards her and a deep sadness at leaving her homeland.

Wang Xijing:
Wang Zhaojun

淡淡裝裳天然樣 西去相知款款訴 褒揚漢匈一家親情同手足地久天長

辛曲暮春悲千里草原綠茵如織 大青山下牛羊遍野中華宇內民族團結情不自禁

頌昭君出塞圖以誌之

王西京於西漢古都長安之未央宮王

SIMA QIAN

Sima Qian (145?-86? B.C.), also called Zichang, was a native of Xiayang (now Hangchen County in Shaanxi Province) during the Western Han Dynasty. He was the most famous historian, prose writer and biographer of ancient China.

Sima Qian was born into an official historian's family. Among the Han people, history and official historians were respected. His dying father asked him to become a grand historian in the palace. "Don't forget the books I wanted to write!" he said.

Sima Qian took an official post and, after a thorough study of Chinese history, wrote *Shi Ji* (*Records of the Historian*), the first comprehensive history book in China. Chinese historians praise the work's rich details, completeness and profound analysis.

Shi Ji covers about 3,000 years, from the beginning of recorded Chinese history to the reign of Emperor Wudi of the Han Dynasty. It includes economics, culture, tribal history and biographies of major figures. It tells of nobles, ordinary people, palace coups and times of peace in a language rivaling great Chinese poetry. Reflecting a progressive outlook, *Shi Ji* stresses the roles all kinds of people play in history.

Sima Qian was over 50 when he finished *Shi Ji*. Its success is due, in part, to his maturity. He travelled and studied while young, and only entered politics in his middle age. Unfortunately he offended the emperor and was sentenced to death. Later this was commuted, and he was given the choice of either paying a large fine or submitting to torture. Too poor to pay, he endured great pain in order to finish his great historical work.

Wang Xijing.
Sima Qian

SU WU

Su Wu (?-60 B.C.) also called Ziqing, was born in Dulin (now Xi'an) during the Western Han Dynasty. His father was a general who made his name fighting the Xiongnu to the north. With his father's help, Su Wu entered the emperor's service at a very young age, and eventually became a national hero.

War broke out between the Han and the Xiongnu after 133 B.C. Both sides distrusted each other and had detained envoys sent to negotiate peace. By 100 B.C. the new ruler of the Xiongnu and Han emperor Wudi both wanted to improve relations. Su Wu was sent in the capacity of Zhonglangjiang (an officer in charge of the emperor's bodyguards) to negotiate. While he was with the Xiongnu, some Han generals who had been captured staged a revolt. Su Wu was suspected of being involved, and was sent to tend sheep in Beihai, now Lake Baikal of the Soviet Union. Beihai was desolate and sparsely populated. Su Wu was given a flock of only male sheep and told he would be sent back to the Han court when the males gave birth to lambs.

Su Wu grew old, but he maintained the dignity of an imperial envoy. He longed to return to the Han court, and refused to join the Xiongnu. Although he drank dirty water and ate grass seeds, he carried his staff of office with pride.

In 90 B.C. the Han emperor sent Li Ling to attack the Xiongnu and rescue Su Wu. But Li Ling was defeated and surrendered. He was sent to convince Su Wu to unite with the Xiongnu. He told Su Wu that his mother and elder brother had died, his wife had remarried, and he himself had almost been forgotton. "Why are you so stubborn?" Li asked. Su Wu replied that a Han official "should be loyal to the emperor like a son to his father..:. I will maintain the spirit of an envoy and will never repent even though I might die."

Su Wu passed 19 years in Beihai tending sheep until 81 B.C. when he was brought back home. The Han people put up colorful lanterns to welcome the old man as a national hero.

Wang Xijing:
Su Wu

ZHANG HENG

Born into a poor family, Zhang Heng (78-139) became one of ancient China's greatest astronomers. He was also called Pingzi and was a native of Nanyang (present-day Henan Province).

At the end of the first century A.D. and the beginning of the second, the Eastern Han Dynasty reached its apex. Economics, culture and transportation were well developed.

In this atmosphere, Zhang Heng studied hard and gained a minor official post when he was 23.

He successfully carried out his responsibilities and also continued his studies, particularly in astronomy and literature. In the second year of the reign of Emperor Andi of the Eastern Han Dynasty, Zhang Heng, then 37, was made Taishilin, an official in charge of astronomical observations and making calendars. This offered him an ideal opportunity to carry out his research on astronomy, geography and lunisolar calendars.

Through painstaking efforts, in 117 he made a bronze armillary sphere, an astronomical instrument which revolved using the power of water poured from pots. With the device he could calculate the rising and setting of the sun and moon with remarkable accuracy. This delicate, complex instrument, built 1,800 years ago, was really a pioneering work in human history. Twenty-one years later, in 138, Zhang Heng made a pneumatic sphere which could detect earthquakes more than 500 km away. It represented an entirely new way of measuring and studying this phenomenon.

Zhang Heng wrote many works. His most famous one, *Linxian*, chronicles his study of the heavenly bodies. In *Linxian* Zhang Heng developed a concept of the universe and explained the source of moonlight and the cause of lunar eclipses. These theories demonstrate the advanced level of Chinese astronomy at that time.

Besides astronomy, Zhang Heng also studied philosophy, literature and poetry. In 1956 Guo Moruo, then President of the Chinese Academy of Sciences, wrote an inscription for a monument honoring Zhang Heng: "A person such as he, cultivated in all the arts, is rare throughout world history."

Wang Mingming:
Zhang Heng

ZHANG ZHONGJING

Zhang Zhonjing (150-219), also called Ji, was known as one of China's greatest doctors.

Born into a well-to-do peasant family, late in the Eastern Han Dynasty in Nanyang, now in Henan Province, Zhang Zhongjing loved to read stories about doctors.

Towards the end of the Eastern Han Dynasty, corruption and frequent wars threw the country into turmoil. Then the nation was hit by a plague, which prompted one poet to write, "White bones lie exposed in the fields; No cocks were heard crowing within a thousand *li*." Zhang Zhongjing witnessed the tragedy and felt the importance of medicine.

He studied very hard, both from books and from famous doctors. His flexibility and creativity made his medical practice a success.

Zhang Zhongjing felt sympathy towards his patients. He accumulated rich experience both in how to cure their illnesses and calm their fears. He constantly studied, improving his skills and recording what he had learned. After a few decades he finished *Treatise on Febrile and Other Diseases*. The book, which details his theories of pathology, dignosis and treatment using traditional Chinese medicine, was partially lost in the subsequent war years. Doctors of later generations tried to recover the lost materials and compiled *Treatise on Febrile Diseases* and *Jingui Collection of Prescriptions*. Both books are still consulted in China.

Zhang Zhongjing was also interested in disease prevention. He believed that "a proper diet, a moderate life and balanced work and rest" are the keys to good health. He also advocated *qigong*, a kind of breathing exercises, and massage to keep fit. Time has proven him to be correct.

Wang Xijing:
Zhang Zhongjing

CAO CAO

A native of Peiguojiao (in present-day Anhui Province), Cao Cao (155-220) was also called Mengde. He was an outstanding politician, military strategist and scholar during the Three Kingdoms period.

Cao Cao remains a mystery in Chinese history. He intimately understood political trickery and was good at using people. No one could understand his thinking. When he was young, some people predicted he would be "an able ruler in times of peace and an arch careerist in times of turbulence". In the eyes of his followers he was awe-inspiring and enigmatic. He turned his neighboring states against each other and later destroyed many feudal lords and unified the northern part of China. He established the kingdom of Wei which, with its rivals the Shu and the Wu, formed the Three Kingdoms after the fall of the Han Dynasty.

Born into a eunuch's family, Cao Cao managed to win the favor of the emperor. But his family background was bad; moreover, he did not have the same surname as the royal family, so Cao Cao never gained a dukedom in spite of his heroic deeds.

During long years of fighting, Cao Cao controlled the emperor and made him issue decrees in his favor. Cao Cao tried to consolidate his power and unify China.

Cao Cao was a great military strategist. He contributed notes for the famous *Sun Zi's Military Tactics*. He knew how to use people, even his enemies.

Cao Cao was also a poet. His writing expresses the hardships of war and his dream to unify China. In *Wanhai (Watching the Sea)* he wrote,

"Autumn wind sighs, the sea surges,
From where the sun and moon rise,
And the stars glitter."

After his death, Cao Cao's second son, Cao Pi, replaced the Han emperor. He posthumously named his father Emperor Wu Di.

Wang Xijing:
Cao Cao

ZHUGE LIANG

Known as Kong Ming, Zhuge Liang (181-234) was a native of Langxie Yangdu (in today's Shandong Province). He was an outstanding statesman and strategist during the Three Kingdoms period. He became a symbol of resourcefulness and wisdom in Chinese folklore.

Throughout Chinese history, the rise of each dynasty depended on military might. Because of this, China is famous for the ancient art of war, which is in fact a branch of ancient Chinese philosophy. The outstanding manual *Sun Zi's Military Tactics* was written during the Spring and Autumn period (770-476 B.C.).

After the Qin and Han Dynasties, which unified China, the nation twice fell into the hands of warlords fighting among themselves. In their scramble for domination, the Wei, Shu and Wu kingdoms were the best at strategies and tactics. It was during this time that Zhuge Liang emerged.

Zhuge Liang was a hermit and did a lot of reading before he became prime minister under Liu Bei, ruler of the Shu Kingdom. Thereafter, he fought bravely for his sovereign. A genius in strategy, he directed Shu military tactics for 26 years. He advised Liu Bei after carefully analysing a situation, and he sometimes commanded troops and directed battles on the field. With his unique talents he helped the Shu Kingdom grow strong and influential.

Zhuge Liang advocated very strict discipline. He said, "Order in marching means victory." He asked his men to share alike in hardship and victory.

Zhuge Liang studied all aspects of military science. In wars he used geography and weather to his advantage.

In 228 he began a vicious struggle with the Wei troops. He died of exhaustion in 234 in a tent, without realizing his ambition of unifying China.

Wang Mingming:
Zhuge Liang

諸葛亮

漢庚辰年
明三寫

CAI YAN

Poet Cai Yan lived during the late Han Dynasty. A native of Chenliuyuan in present-day Henan Province, she also called herself Wenji.

Cai Yan was influenced by her father, a well-known scholar and calligrapher who was well-versed in history, music and astronomy.

When her first husband died during the war-torn years of the late Han Dynasty, she returned to her own family. She was captured by followers of Dong Zhuo, who married her to King Zuoxian of the Xiongnu in the north.

Twelve years later, in 208, Cao Cao, prime minister of the Han Dynasty, was recruiting talented advisors. He missed Cai Yan's knowledgeable father and sent a small expedition to bring his daughter back.

But Cai Yan was already a mother of two children. She was grateful for the chance to return, but she hated to part with her two children. After agonizing over the choice, she decided to leave them. On her way back home she wrote with sorrow, "On leaving home I missed home; On coming back I cry to leave my children."

Later Cao Cao helped her to marry a Han general, Dong Si. But she could never forget her two children. Her five-character poem *Beifen Shi (A Poem on Grief and Indignation)* described her experience. She also authored *Hujia Shibapai (Eighteen-Rhythm Music for Hujia)*.

Cai Yan's fate reflected the social position of women in her time. She is remembered in history and literature as a talented woman who sacrificed her children for her country.

Wang Xijing:
Cai Yan

GE HONG

A Taoist theoretician and doctor, Ge Hong (284-364), also called Baopuzi, was a native of Jiangsu. He is famous for producing "immortality pills"

Ge Hong began his search for immortality pills while in his teens. When he reached 30 he had completed a book called *Baopuzi*, the first medical book in China. It discusses herbal medicine and the theory and techniques of making immortality pills. It became the main guide for others seeking the pills.

People in ancient times tried to extract the essense of immortality from plants or minerals. Most of these experimenters were Taoists and worshipped Lao Zi and Zhuang Zi. At first, Ge Hong really believed in the elixir and planned to make one by transforming minerals. This was the beginning of chemistry.

In the course of his research, Ge Hong was startled to discover that all the materials experienced natural changes and took on different colors at different temperatures. He recorded his observations in his book *Huang-Bai (Yellow-White)*, "Iron becomes red like copper if coated with copper ore."

Baopuzi chronicles Ge Hong's long search for immortality pills He experimented with cinnabar, realgar, alum, sulphur and other elements. Using heat, distillation and other methods, he studied the chemical changes these substances underwent.

Starting from an abstraction, Ge Hong compiled a lot of practical scientific knowledge. Later generations remembered him as a Taoist theoretician and as a talented chemist.

Wang Xijing:
Ge Hong

葛洪炼丹图 记晋著名化学家葛洪炼丹制药故事 辛巳年写於古都长安

WANG XIZHI

Wang Xizhi (321-379), who called himself Yishao, was a native of Linyi (in Shandong Province). He was a great calligrapher during the Eastern Jin Dynasty, and was also known as Wang the Right Army, because he was the general of that unit.

When he was a child, Wang Xizhi stuttered, and was shunned by his parents. Perhaps because of this defect, he preferred calligraphy, expressing his emotions in each stroke of the brush.

Wang Xizhi inherited the plain style of the ancient official script, *lishu*, and had a good command of regular script and the cursive hand. People said his calligraphy looked like "floating clouds and, sometimes, like a startled dragon." His style is still imitated by admirers today.

Chinese characters took their form from simple pictures of stars, clouds, mountains, rivers, birds and other objects in nature. This gives them a direct relationship with the natural world. Calligraphers use form and space to make words touching, forceful and artistic. The Chinese brush creates dots and thick or thin strokes to express the calligrapher's intentions.

Wang Xizhi's simple, romantic calligraphy enchanted Emperor Taizong of the Tang Dynasty. The ruler loved Wang's free yet restrained style and wrote down his praise, "His points and strokes are like clouds which never fade."

Wang Xijing:
Wang Xizhi

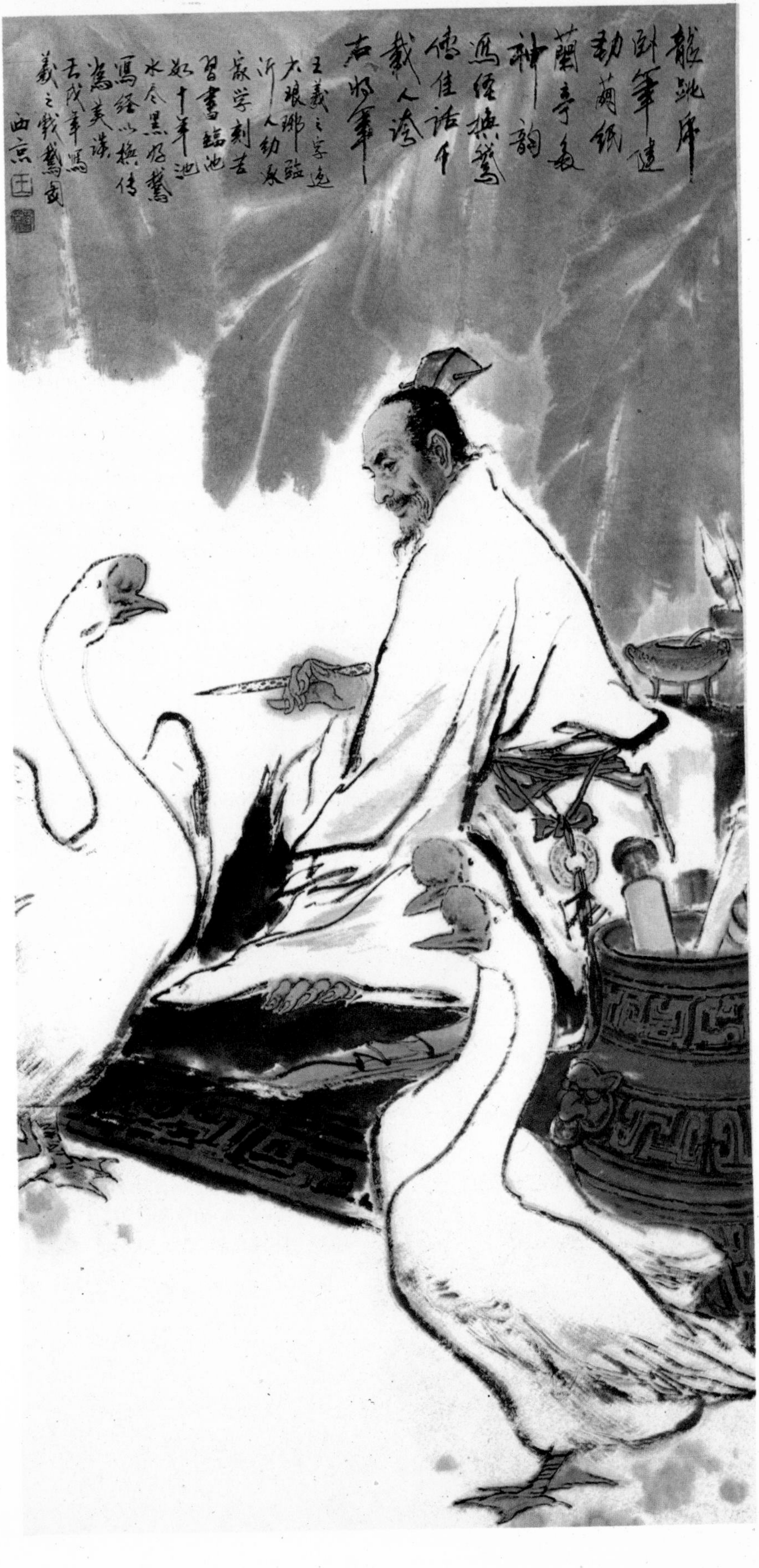

TAO YUANMING

Tao Yuanming (365-427), a noted poet during the Eastern Jin dynasty, was a native of Xunyang Chaishang (now Xingzi County in Jiangxi Province). Born into a declined landlord-bureaucrat family, Tao Yuanming received classical education in Confucianism to prepare him for an imperial appointment. But later, seeing the corruption of the court after a few terms of office, he returned to till his land.

Most of Tao Yuanming's poems were written after he returned to the countryside. They praise work in the fields, freeing him from the cares of officialdom. Some of his poems recall his youthful ambition and bemoan his loneliness. The interplay of ambition and loneliness troubled him all his life, yet they were the keys to his success as a writer. Their complicated relationship laid the foundations for his writing *Taohuayuan Shi (A Poem of the Land of Peach Blossoms)*, in which he describes an ideal society.

Taohuayuan is a beautiful land inhabited by honest, industrious people. Work is filled with happiness. Nature and humanity cooperate. Tao Yuanming used sarcasm and criticism of the world around him to describe his ideal.

He believed he could talk to the plants and animals around him, and could hear them conversing among themselves. He recreated this dialogue in his descriptions of cosy, remote villages, smoking rubble, alleys where dogs barked and mulberry tree orchards where cocks crowed. His images are very natural, real and forceful.

The *fu* poetry of the Han Dynasty depicted nature as an arena where people did good deeds. Mountains and rivers provided backgrounds against which to praise heroes. During the Wei and Jin Dynasties, life was studied from a philosophical angle, along with nature which was regarded as a reflection of human nature. People did this in order to discover a different logic or law. Nature was used to stir up deep thoughts. Tao Yuanming's feeling for nature reflected this social significance.

Tao Yuanming's poems greatly influenced later generations of writers including the famous poets Li Bai and Du Fu.

Wang Xijing:
Tao Yuanming

XIE LINGYUN

Xie Lingyun (385-433), a native of Huiji (present-day Shaoxing in Zhejiang Province), was a poet of the Southern Dynasties.

During the previous Eastern Jin Dynasty, the Xies were a big family of officials in southern China. Xie Lingyun loved to read, and later he became a minor official. He lost favor with his superior and was exiled to another province. He spent the rest of his life wandering around the country, writing poems about mountains and rivers and songs to the sun and the moon.

Wherever he went, hundreds of his faithful followers accompanied him, dressed in bright clothes. The wooden "Xie sandals" he wore when climbing mountains became synonymous with wanderers. Li Bai, a great Tang Dynasty poet, wrote,

"The place Xie stayed still stands;
Where river ripples and monkeys cry.
In Xie sandals, I climb the steps into the clouds;
I see the sun rising from the sea, and hear the heavenly cocks crow."

Xie Lingyun especially loved to describe his reactions to mountains and rivers. These feelings were often fleeting, and he hurried to record them on paper. Many of his lines are still remembered and recited today, although he wrote few poems. Some of his poems are so moving that they create an ache.

"The bright moon shines over the snow on land,
The sunset glows with beauty,
And the calm Cheng River is like a silk ribbon."

Xie Lingyun was the first poet to write extensively about landscapes and is called the father of landscape poets. Although his poems lack any ideological content, his profound descriptions inspired poets of later generations.

Wang Mingming:
Xie Lingyun

SUN SIMIAO

Sun Simiao (581-682) was an outstanding doctor during the Tang Dynasty.

The economy and culture of the early Tang were highly developed. The sons of nobles and rich families studied diligently to prepare for the imperial examinations. Those who wanted to be officials looked down upon doctors. But Sun Simiao suffered from poor health and exhausted his money by visiting doctors. This painful experience left him determined to study medicine.

Sun Simiao was clever and diligent. He soon had a good command of ancient medical theory and practice. His skills were so famous that even Emperor Wendi of the Sui Dynasty and Emperors Taizong and Gaozong of the Tang Dynasty offered him official medical posts. But he turned them all down.

In practicing medicine Sun Simiao showed great sympathy for his patients, even lepers. Treating all of his patients like family, he was unconcerned about collecting fees.

Sun Simiao made careful notes and compiled his experience in physiology, pathology, treatment, prescriptions, accupuncture and massage into a book called *For Emergencies*. He spent the next 30 years preparing *Prescriptions*, which revised and enriched his first book.

In *Prescriptions*, Sun detailed his knowledge of pediatrics, gynecology, treatment, herbs, and prescriptions. He made outstanding contributions to the development of Chinese medicine.

Wang Xijing:
Sun Simiao

WU ZETIAN

Wu Zetian (624-705), the wife of Emperor Gaozong of the Tang Dynasty, later became Empress Wuzhou, the first empress of China. She called herself Zhao and was born in Wenshui, Shanxi Province.

Wu Zetian was brought to the palace by Emperor Taizong when she was 14, winning his favor with her liveliness. He had no idea that she would become as powerful as he in 690.

Emperor Taizong had a wild horse whom nobody could harness. Wu Zetian told him she could accomplish the task with an iron whip, an iron hammer and a dagger. If the horse was still unharnessed after she used the iron whip and hammer, she would use the dagger to cut its throat. Later in her political career, she ruled the court with an iron hand.

The Tang Dynasty had been peaceful and powerful, but the infighting which brought her to power created some political instability. She encouraged people to inform against her detractors. She greatly weakened the opposition, but her iron-handed policy was unpopular. Facing an indignant populace, she ordered that those who had implemented her orders be publicly tortured and condemned. In this way she shifted the responsibility onto her subordinates.

However, Wu Zetian was knowledgeable and a good ruler. She never showed favoritism, not even toward her children. She had worshippers in the court, but she did not allow them to form an influential sect. Those who were loyal to her could count on her help in times of trouble. And she refused to believe any slanderous accusations. Under these policies, her government operated normally, free from infighting, rebellion and foreign aggression, until her death in 705.

The empress' greatest innovation gave nobles, landlords and even the common people a chance to become officials through various measures, including "self-recommendation." Meanwhile, she used the law to punish the incompetent, sometimes killing whole clans.

Because Wu Zetian kept China unified and open to the world, the Tang Dynasty under her rule was affluent and powerful. Although she came to the throne by foul means, people saw her as shrewd, capable and far-sighted.

Wang Mingming:
Wu Zetian

武則天造像

歲次辛巳月

明畫

ZHANG RUOXU

Zhang Ruoxu (660-720), a native of Yangzhou, was a famous poet during the early Tang Dynasty.

Little is known about his life, but his representative work, *Spring Flowers and River in the Moonlight*, is still admired today. The poem is likened to a bright moon shining over the long river of Chinese literature.

The best Chinese poems were written during the Tang Dynasty. In the early part, when Zhang lived, great changes were taking place. Family backgrounds and relationships, which used to be stressed in marriage, were replaced by the value of individuals. People were encouraged to seek official posts. For landlord families with no hereditary titles, the surest way to officialdom was to join the army and be sent to the frontiers. Therefore, there were many, many people who took an official post and did something beneficial for the country. Most were inspired by stories of heroes to practice martial arts and join the army to protect the borders. This also became part of the romantic experience of the poets. Zhang wrote,

"Tasty grape wine shines in my glass;
I was about to drink to the *pipa* music,
When the horse was spurred to leave.
Don't laugh at me who got drunk on the battlefield,
Since ancient times how many people have come back from war?"

Zhang Ruoxu lived during this exciting, hopeful time, but felt somewhat perplexed by his future. Looking across the river into the distance under a bright moon, he wrote,

"Who saw the moon first?
What year did it first light the people?
There will be no end to generations,
And the moon will appear the same for ever.
But who is the moon waiting for?
I see only the Changjiang bringing water here."

The beauty of the poem comes from its sadness. Zhang was young and puzzled when he wrote it. But it is a sweet, bewildering sadness, not dim or depressed. The Tang poets after Zhang continued this theme of expectant uncertainty over the future.

Wang Mingming:
Zhang Ruoxu

WANG WEI

A noted Tang Dynasty musician, painter and poet, Wang Wei (701-761) called himself Moji and was a native of Taiyuanqi (present-day Qixian County in Shanxi).

Wang Wei was very gifted at an early age. When he was just 21, he passed the imperial examination and was given an official position as musician. He wrote many lines and composed many songs which were sung throughout the country.

In the 24th year under the reign of Emperor Kaiyuan of the Tang Dynasty (736), the prime minister Zhang Jiuling, a good man, was falsely accused for political reasons and was dismissed from office. Li Linfu, an unscrupulous man, gained control of the court. The change destroyed Wang Wei's political ambitions. He became depressed and devoted himself to writing poetry.

Wang Wei's poems and articles were considered the best at the time. His descriptions of mountains and rivers were the most impressive. He composed his images carefully, like a painter. The world under his pen moved and hummed with life. He regarded nature with great reverence, as in *Bird Singing Stream*.

"People pause, osmanthus flowers fall,
Night is still, the spring mountain is deserted.
The moon gone, mountain birds are startled,
By the spring stream they sometimes sing."

In his late years Wang Wei lived in a villa owned by another poet. It was a quiet place, skirted by a stream and with a small plot of bamboos and some flower beds. He sang, "So many sad things I have encountered in my life, I can tell no one but the monks." He often went boating with his friends, playing music for them and reciting poems. Later he gathered all of his landscape poems into *A Collection from Wangchuan*.

Wang Wei is a bright star in the history of Chinese literature. A versatile artist, he wrote music, poetry and was an impressive painter. His work greatly influenced later generations.

Wang Mingming:
Wang Wei

獨坐幽篁裏彈琴復長嘯
深林人不知明月來相照
王維詩意 歲在庚辰
秋於賓虹夜畫屋

LI BAI

Li Bai (701-762), also called Taibai, inherited and developed the romantic tradition of Qu Yuan to become one of the greatest Tang Dynasty poets.

Born into a wealthy merchant family, Li Bai spent his childhood in a frontier area and later moved to Sichuan with his father. At that time, the Tang Dynasty was in its heyday.

As a boy, Li Bai was vivacious and a clever writer. At 15 he took up swordplay. At 20 he often visited hermits and Taoist monks, and at 26 he left home to visit China's famous mountains and scenic spots.

Li Bai became famous for his poetry when he was only a boy. His poems were known for their romanticism. He created quite a stir and was invited to the court. But soon after he arrived, he found he was merely an unusual decoration.

Disillusioned, he left the court two years later, forever changed. Li Bai saw a new world in nature where everything was not an illusion. Nature's struggle for existence was more difficult than for humans. With a heavy heart, Li Bai became a wandering hermit.

He began his second trip around the country after he left the Tang capital. The poems Li Bai wrote at that time were bold yet full of loneliness. In 758, when the poet was 57, he was exiled in Yelang (present-day Guizhou) because of his involvement in some political infighting. Two years later he was reunited with his family in Jiangxi, his hometown. He died two years later.

Li Bai is one of the most highly regarded poets in Chinese literature. *Works of Li Taibai* includes more than 900 poems, all revealing his mastery of the romanitc tradition. His impact on later writers is immeasurable.

Wang Xijing:
Li Bai

DU FU

Du Fu (712-770), like Li Bai, was one of the greatest poets of the Tang Dynasty. He named himself Zimei and was a native of Xianyang (now Xianfang in Hubei Province).

Du Fu lived during the Tang Dynasty's slow decline. In the turbulent society, class and racial conflicts were acute and the average person led a miserable life. Of course, this was reflected in the literature of the day. Li Bai's romantic optimism gave way to Du Fu's realism.

Du Fu combined the brilliant insight of a scholar with the sensitive practicality of a common man. He showed no confidence in Buddhism or Taoism. He was reluctant to go wandering around the country, cutting himself off from the state and the people.

Du Fu was honest and poor as a young man and failed to get an influential official post. His life was often unstable and poor. When he reached middle age, the An-Shi Revolt (755) broke out. Years of bitter war left agriculture in ruins and many people homeless. The central government was weakened and regional lords each grabbed for their share.

Deeply grieved, Du Fu wrote some lines which have been handed down through history.

> "Country torn yet the mountains and rivers are still there,
> Fallen cities are strewn with wild grass.
> When moved the flowers are tearful,
> Hateful I am startled by birds."

He was moved by all the suffering around him and felt powerless to change the tide. His warm concern for the people is clear.

Because of his practical attitude, Du Fu had wide social contacts. He was thus able to record the decline of the Tang Dynasty, the devastating An-Shi Revolt, the acute contradictions between the landlords and peasants, social habits and landscapes in his poetry. He inherited and perfected the literary tradition of realism which began with the publication of the *Book of Songs*. His compassionate realism stands beside the bold romanticism of Li Bai's poems like two exquisite flowers of the Tang Dynasty.

Wang Xijing:
Du Fu

国破山河在城春草木深感时花溅泪恨别鸟惊心烽火连三月家书抵万金白头搔更短浑欲不胜簪杜甫春望之意壬戌年初夏于西京写于长安杜石樵

YANG GUIFEI

Yang Guifei (719-756), also called Yuhuan, was the favorite concubine of Emperor Xuanzong of the Tang Dynasty. In 745 the ruler named her Guifei, which means favorite concubine. She was a native of Yongle in Yangpu Prefecture in present-day Shanxi Province.

The story about Yang Guifei and Empror Xuanzong, who was on the throne between 712-756, was so popular during the Tang Dynasty that Yang Guifei appeared in poems of several very famous poets, including Bai Juyi, Du Fu, Li Shanying and Su Shi. Some depicted how she was brought to court and managed to win the emperor's favor, and others said her charms over the emperor made him shirk his duties. Verses also recounted the sovereign's torment when she died a tragic death. The poets tried to link the decline of the once-powerful dynasty with the beauty who enchanted the ruler.

In the 713-741 period, the Tang Dynasty reached its height after about a century of development. Emperor Xuanzong had been on the throne for more than 30 years. Most of his goals had been fulfilled, except his search for an extraordinarily beautiful women. Gao Lishi, a eunuch who was also his bailiff, recommended a girl named Yang Yuhuan. The emperor fell in love with her at first sight. In Bai Juyi's poem, she "looked back with a charming smile, making all the cosmetics lose their color." Yang Yuhuan was a very good dancer and singer. Her *Feather Dress Dance* caused a stir at the court. People of later generations said there were "3,000 beauties in the rear palace, yet only one won favor of the emperor."

The emperor became obsessed with Yang Yuhuan's dancing and singing. Sometimes he played musical instruments for her. An Lushan, who was later involved in the An-Shi Revolt, also won favor of the emperor with a kind of frenetic dance.

In the meantime, the emperor promoted the Yang family. Yang Guozhong, Yang Yuhuan's distant brother, was a devious man, but was appointed prime minister.

In 755, An Lushan started a rebellion. Emperor Xuanzong was caught unprepared. The rebels took advantage of the emperor's fatuousness and moved very quickly. Next year the emperor fled Chang'an together with Yang Guifei. When they reached Maweiyi (present-day Wuping County in Shanxi Province), the troops following the emperor rebelled and killed Yang Guozhong. They surrounded the emperor's camp and demanded the death of Yang Guifei. The ruler ordered her killed. She hung herself in a pear tree at the age of 37.

"A branch of pear flowers in the spring rain" is how Bai Juyi described Emperor Xuanzong's dream of Yang Guifei. In Bai Juyi's poem, she was as pure as a pear flower sprinkled with raindrops. Like many other women in the palace, Yang Guifei enjoyed an unusually luxurious life and eventually fell victim to it.

Wang Xijing:
Yang Guifei

贵妃簪花图

壬戌年仲秋写於古長安華清池畔

王西京

HUAI SU

The noted calligrapher Huai Su (725-785), a native of Changsha in Hunan, was also a monk. His real name was Qian.

Huai Su's calligraphy style was known as "crazy grass." According to legend, he learned how to write with a bald brush. When he was young, he was so poor that he used palm tree leaves as paper. Huai Su was an alcoholic, but he wrote better and more fluently when drunk.

A fluid and unrestrained style was popular in all arts during the prosperous Tang Dynasty. The vigorous, romantic spirit of the times, expressed in the line "Tasty grape wine shines in my glass," influenced traditional "line art" to become more poetic.

Ancient pottery and bronze wares, calligraphy, paintings and other arts were constantly developing to express new ideas. In calligraphy, changes in the lines together with a flowing style became the standard of beauty and, finally, formed the artistic tradition of the Chinese culture.

The calligraphy of Huai Su captured the flavor of the flourishing Tang Dynasty. His lines reflect the changing emotions of calligraphers as the official *lishu* script was replaced by a free *xingshu* script. The calligraphy of Huai Su represents the new, vivid style.

Wang Xijing:
Huai Su

LIU YUXI

Liu Yuxi (772-842), also called Mengde, was a native of Luyang in Henan. He was an outstanding poet of the mid-Tang Dynasty and a materialist thinker as well.

Born into a bureaucratic family, Liu Yuxi held an official post from an early age. But his outspoken and straightforward style earned him only demotions. He had such a long disappointing career that Bai Juyi, a late Tang poet, wrote, "Too many ups and downs in 23 years." At this time, Liu Yuxi, living in a small town, Yangzhou, was moved by Bai's lines and wrote,

"Desolate as the Ba Mountain and the Chu River,
Where I was left for 23 years.
A thousand sails pass by the shipwreck,
Ten thousand saplings shoot up beyond the withered tree.
Hearing your singing today,
I now depend on cups of wine to raise my spirits."

When he was brought back to the capital, Chang'an, he remained frank. He looked down on those who condemned him and lost favor with the court again.

Liu Yuxi's poems were relatively restrained and neutral; hence, they were regarded as mature. Because of his expriences, he was able to write with feeling about nature.

"Mountain peach flowers turn the peak crimson,
The Shu River licks the foot of the mountain.
The reddening flowers wither easily like a man's love,
The river flows endlessly like the flow of my troubles."

The *Collection of Liu Mengde's Poems*, still popular today, preserves many of his verses.

Wang Mingming:
Liu Yuxi

BAI JUYI

Another famous Tang Dynasty poet, Bai Juyi (772-846) used a style different from the two greats, Li Bai and Du Fu. He called himself Letian and was a native of Xinchengxian in Henan.

Bai Juyi's honesty and openness brought him nothing but trouble as a court official.

In writing, he rejected the idea of pure artistic form in favor of a literature accessible to the people. Many of his poems describe the life of poor people, including old women and peasants. His famous poems *Qinzhong Yin* and *Xin Yuefu* are said to have made the nobles of Chang'an "change colours" and "look at each other."

Bai Juyi hid his artistic style in objective description. He wrote,

"Dry wind blows in rainless March,
  Wheat stops sprouting and dies in the fields."
"Strip me of my clothes,
  Grab food from my mouth."

The lines are far from elegant, but they expose the suffering of the people.

As a realistic poet, Bai Juyi examined his environment coldly. This made his poems clear, terse and easily understandable. His ideas were never rigidly expressed or over-explained.

His *Song of Deep Hatred* tells of the love between Emperor Xuanzong and Yang Guifei from a historical point of view. It is representative of Bai Juyi's work, and is considered a classic of Chinese literature.

Bai Juyi's poems are still loved today by people from all walks of life.

Wang Mingming:
Bai Juyi

琵琶行

浔阳江头夜送客，枫叶荻花秋瑟瑟。主人下马客在船，举酒欲饮无管弦。醉不成欢惨将别，别时茫茫江浸月。忽闻水上琵琶声，主人忘归客不发。寻声暗问弹者谁，琵琶声停欲语迟。移船相近邀相见，添酒回灯重开宴。千呼万唤始出来，犹抱琵琶半遮面。转轴拨弦三两声，未成曲调先有情。弦弦掩抑声声思，似诉平生不得志。低眉信手续续弹，说尽心中无限事。轻拢慢捻抹复挑，初为霓裳后六幺。大弦嘈嘈如急雨，小弦切切如私语。嘈嘈切切错杂弹，大珠小珠落玉盘。间关莺语花底滑，幽咽泉流水下滩。水泉冷涩弦凝绝，凝绝不通声暂歇。别有幽愁暗恨生，此时无声胜有声。银瓶乍破水浆迸，铁骑突出刀枪鸣。曲终收拨当心画，四弦一声如裂帛。东船西舫悄无言，唯见江心秋月白。

沉吟放拨插弦中，整顿衣裳起敛容。自言本是京城女，家在虾蟆陵下住。十三学得琵琶成，名属教坊第一部。曲罢曾教善才服，妆成每被秋娘妒。五陵年少争缠头，一曲红绡不知数。钿头银篦击节碎，血色罗裙翻酒污。今年欢笑复明年，秋月春风等闲度。弟走从军阿姨死，暮去朝来颜色故。门前冷落鞍马稀，老大嫁作商人妇。商人重利轻别离，前月浮梁买茶去。去来江口守空船，绕船月明江水寒。夜深忽梦少年事，梦啼妆泪红阑干。

我闻琵琶已叹息，又闻此语重唧唧。同是天涯沦落人，相逢何必曾相识。我从去年辞帝京，谪居卧病浔阳城。浔阳地僻无音乐，终岁不闻丝竹声。住近湓江地低湿，黄芦苦竹绕宅生。其间旦暮闻何物，杜鹃啼血猿哀鸣。春江花朝秋月夜，往往取酒还独倾。岂无山歌与村笛，呕哑嘲哳难为听。今夜闻君琵琶语，如听仙乐耳暂明。莫辞更坐弹一曲，为君翻作琵琶行。感我此言良久立，却坐促弦弦转急。凄凄不似向前声，满座重闻皆掩泣。座中泣下谁最多，江州司马青衫湿。

读白居易琵琶行而作此图记之 顺德范曾

LIU ZONGYUAN

Liu Zongyuan (773-819), who called himself Zihou, is traditionally recognized as a principal leader of the "guwen" (classical Chinese) movement during the Tang Dynasty and an outstanding essayist and poet. He was also a materialist and a political reformist.

Liu Zongyuan was born into a landlord family which owned several hectares of land and several hundred fruit trees. His mother was a typical ancient Chinese woman — gentle, intelligent, diligent and strict in abiding by the clan rules. Influenced by his highly educated mother, Liu Zongyuan, a brilliant young man, passed the highest imperial examination at the age of 21 and immediately proved himself to be smart, upright and fearless. He wrote some materialistic philosophical works such as *On Candles* and *On Heaven*.

In 805 a series of reforms which Liu Zongyuan had supported failed. He fell from imperial favor and was given a minor official post. During this period he wrote many short fables of deep social significance. *The Snake-Catcher*, for example, tells of a villager who had to risk his life to catch snakes in order to pay his land tax and other levies. It implied that for the poor people taxes were as ferocious and ruthless as poisonous snakes.

Liu Zongyuan endeared himself to Chinese readers for centuries with his descriptions of scenic landscapes. Reflecting his own tenacity, he described mountains and rivers vividly in his poetry. The highly-praised *Eight Notes in Yongzhou*, in contrast with traditional poems of despair, is picturesque and realistic.

Liu Zongyuan was finally sent to remote Liuzhou (in present-day Guangxi). Instead of losing heart, he was determined to help the local people. His greatest achievement there was to liberate slaves. He banished the local system of selling girls.

Liu Zongyuan's policies put the people first, and he was warmly supported. In three years, great changes took place in Liuzhou. The local people were very grateful to him and swiftly carried out his programs.

After his death, the Liuzhou people built a temple in his honor. A tomb containing his hat and clothes still stands. His friend Liu Yuxie collected and published his writings in *The Poetry of Liuhedong*.

Wang Mingming:
Liu Zongyuan

LI HE

A distinguished poet of the late Tang Dynasty, Li He (790-816), also known as Changjie, was a native of Changgu (in present-day Henan Province).

Li He was born into a poor family. He was noted for his talent and virtues from early childhood, but an ancient superstition barred him from the highest imperial examination, called "jinshi." Li He's father was named Li Jinshu, and ancient custom forbids a person to use any part of the given name of an ancestor. Because the "jin" of "jinshi" is pronounced similar to the "jin" of his father's name "Jinshu," Li He never took the test. He died at the age of 26.

Li He's poetry can be compared with that of Li Bai and Du Fu. However, Li He was not as influential in his own time as these other great poets. Though young and gifted, he had to resign himself to relative obscurity. Disappointed, he was moody and changeable, with a rich but eccentric imagination.

In writing poetry, Li He used color to mobilize his emotions, while other poets used color only to highlight feelings. With a heavy heart, Li He wrote,

"Covered with black clouds,
The town seemed to collapse.
Under white moonlight,
Armor suits shone brightly."

The beautiful scene did not ease his deep depression.

"I am not able to call any lingering spirit back;
When the cock crows, all under heaven is bright."

Thin, weak and sentimental, Li He looked handsome and troubled. He travelled by donkey, always thinking of how to express himself. Wherever he thought of a good line he wrote it down and tossed it in his bag. At home in the evenings, he took out his notes and put them in order. Once when his mother was looking through his bag, she exclaimed in surprise, "My boy! You'll work your heart out!"

Li He continued the romantic tradition of Qu Yuan and Li Bai. Noted for his mythological poems, he was called an eccentric poet. *The Poetry of Li He* includes 223 works.

Wang Xijing:
Li He

AUNT GONGSUN

Aunt Gongsun was a Tang Dynasty dancer, famous for her exciting sword dances. Du Fu, the noted Tang poet, witnessed her performance and wrote a well-known poem, *Watching Aunt Gongsun and Her Disciples Doing Sword Dances,* in 767.

Du Fu's poem describes her popular, soul-stirring performance. When Aunt Gongsun swung her sword, light flashed in all directions. Her elegant and vigorous movements resembled a group of immortals riding flying dragons.

To drumbeats, Aunt Gongsun moved strongly and as fast as lightning. Suddenly she stopped gracefully, like a beacon shining over the sea. Her audiences were stunned by this powerful contrast.

Sword dancing probably developed from the swordplay of Chinese martial arts. A dancer holds two swords or a sword and a silk scarf. The dancer's beautiful costume presents a noble bearing. According to Du Fu, Aunt Gongsun looked very beautiful in satin clothes. Because people loved her dancing, her costumes became fashionable with young women.

Chinese martial arts have a long history. Used both for self-defense and to improve health, the main schools use swordplay, boxing, knives, spears, cudgels and whips. Sword dancing suits women, requiring both gentleness and firmness. The performer's sword style shows her heroic spirit.

Wang Xijing:
Aunt Gongsun

DU MU

Du Mu(803-853),who called himself Muzhi,was a native of Wannian(present-day Xi'an). He was a celebrated scholar of the late Tang Dynasty.

Du Mu was born into a declined aristocratic family. A gifted boy, he read history books and studied military strategy and tactics. When he was only 20, he wrote *The Poem of Epang Palace*. The beautiful rhythms of this poem, reflecting his unique spirit, make it a literary masterpiece even today. When he was 26, Du Mu passed his imperial examination and became an advisor to the emperor. Like other scholars and officials, Du Mu worked hard for the government and to advance his career. He also enjoyed the luxurious life of an aristocrat. When he was assistant to the local official in Yangzhou, he worked during the day and pursued a life of pleasure at night. Later he recalled humorously, "I had a 10-year dream in Yangzhou. What I gained is a bad reputation for visiting brothels."

Gentle yet firm, Du Mu was not overly serious about his political career. He suffered some setbacks but was never entirely discredited. He advanced to writing documents for the emperor before he died at the age of 50.

Du Mu wrote in gentle, slow rhythms, never revealing his inner feelings. His work reflects his aristocratic, leisurely manner and carelessness. His poems are humorous and metaphorical.

"Smoke envelops cold water and moonlight covers the earth,
I anchor my boat at night near a wineshop by the Qinhuai River.
The girl singer does not grieve over loss of country,
Still singing across the river 'Back Chamber Flower'."

In the late Tang Dynasty, Du Mu and Li Shangyin enjoyed equal popularity. They were called "the lesser Li and Du," a pun on Li Bai and Du Fu. Du Mu was one of the few carefree poets of that time. His verses, noted for their clear and beautiful language, are still admired and respected.

Wang Xijing:
Du Mu

LI SHANGYIN

Another celebrated poet of the late Tang Dynasty, Li Shangyin (813-858) called himself Yishan.

Li Shangyin was the son of a junior official. Because his father died when he was young, Li Shangyin grew reserved and mature at an early age. He passed the imperial examinations when he was 25, and served various governors in different parts of China.

During the late Tang Dynasty, two factions, the Niu and the Li, feuded. Li Shangyin, a member of the Niu group but married to a girl whose father served the Li, refused to take sides. Annoying both factions, Li's official career stalled.

He wrote many poems, greatly influencing later poets. Most of his works address his contemporary socio-political situation. Other untitled works deal mainly with clandestine love.

Love is one of the major subjects of traditional Chinese poetry. *Shi Jing (Book of Songs)*, the oldest book of poetry, contains vivid, lively love poems. Chinese love poems feature unique characteristics. The love poems written by Li Shangyin stand out.

"Hard for us to meet, even harder to part with each other;
East wind blows weakly while blossoms fall.
Silkworms spin silk until they die;
Tears will not dry until the candle is burnt out."

Li Shangyin's attitude towards love differed from his contemporaries, such as Du Mu. Du Mu wrote lyric poetry to express his feelings when he was in love or when he was thwarted in his political career. However, Li Shangyin thought that love was an entity, containing its own beautiful and noble things. He believed one must work hard to obtain true love. This outlook gave his love poems their special style.

Worried about personal and political problems, Li Shangyin often felt lonely even in happy situations. However, this loneliness was transformed by his sensitive talent into brilliant writing.

"As autumn clouds do not disperse,
Frost comes later,
Only leaving dead lotuses listening to the sounds of rain."
"How nice the setting sun is,
but it is near dusk."

Later generations know little of Li's personal life. But his poetry, with its beautiful lines and elaborate verbal and tonal patterns, testifies to his considerable talent.

Wang Mingming:
Li Shangyin

WANG ANSHI

Wang Anshi (1021-1085), also called Banshan or Jiefu, was a renowned politician, thinker and writer of the Northern Song Dynasty.

In his youth, Wang Anshi followed his father, an official, who moved all over the country. Experienced and knowledgeable, he was not rigid and narrow-minded as those who came from feudal families. He studied the works of Confucius and other scholars, as well as unofficial history books and stories. He preferred to analyze and solve problems on his own, without the help of commentaries. After passing his imperial examination at the age of 22, Wang Anshi began his official career.

In 1069, Emperor Shenzong, a determined reformer, put Wang Anshi in charge of his reform program. Wang had already won a reputation among his seniors for his intellectual competence. The next year he became the prime minister and spread change far and wide. These reforms included programs for land measurement, taxation, equitable distribution aimed at price control, labor service exemption, irrigation works and reorganizatin of the armed forces. Under his leadership, new rules and regulations on state administration, imperial examinations and education were also established.

In the course of this reform, Wang Anshi displayed remarkable competence in drawing up systematic theories and concrete plans. He wrote the well-known *A Reply to Sima Guang's Memorial*. Sima Guang became prime minister after Emperor Shenzong died, and strongly opposed Wang Anshi's reforms. In his reply, Wang was neither arrogant nor servile in defending his programs, and expressed his determination to carry them out. He attacked Sima Guang's criticisms directly, showing that he was a mature politician with a strong, analytical and quick mind.

But Sima Guang gained the upper hand politically, and the reforms were cancelled. Wang Anshi was forced to resign and went back to his hometown of Jiangning (present-day Nanjing).

By then Wang Anshi was already quite old, and chose a quiet place to build his house. He named it Banshan Garden, and wrote many poems and essays describing the daily life of the villagers and the beautiful landscape. His poetry is lucid and lively. The plain, succinct and fresh language conveys Wang Anshi's unbreakable spirit.

Younger generations of writers have seriously studied his analytical methods and his impressive use of language. *The Collected Works of Wang Anshi* is widely read today.

Wang Mingming:
Wang Anshi

SHEN KUO

Song Dynasty scientist and politician Shen Kuo (1031-1095), who called himself Cunzhong, was a native of Qiantang County (now Hangzhou in Zhejiang Province).

Shen Kuo began his official career at the age of 24 and passed the highest imperial examination at 33. He supported Wang Anshi's reforms, and lost his post when the movement failed. He settled down in the Dream Brook Garden in Runzhou (now Zhengjiang).

Knowledgeable and talented, he studied astronomy, geography, mathematics, physics, chemistry, biology, medicine, water conservation, military strategy, literature and music. He wrote several dozen books; the most oustanding is *Sketches and Notes in Mengxi*, a well-known encyclopedic work both at home and abroad. Later he also wrote *Supplement to Sketches and Notes* and *Continuation of Sketches and Notes*.

Many of Shen Kuo's scientific achievements predated the same discoveries in Western countries. For example, he once pointed out, "We sharpen magnetite to make a compass; however, a compass often declines slightly to the east instead of pointing exactly to the south." He discovered magnetic declination more than 400 years earlier than Columbus did on his famous voyage in 1492.

Shen Kuo inspected the area at the foot of Taihang Mountain in 1074. When he found a layer covered with snail shells and pebbles, he asserted, "It is an ancient seashore." By inference, he continued, "Continents' inland plains were actually formed by alluvial soil." Six hundred years later, a British scholar put forward the same theory.

In his later years, Shen Kuo worked out a 12-month, four-season calender. His calendar is more accurate than the first one made by a British astronomer.

Though absorbed by his scientific research, Shen Kuo always mingled with the working people and learned what he could from them. He once said, "Tools and instruments, the measure system and color were not invented by educated people. The strength of artisans, workers and farmers has never been counted."

Understanding the impact of common people was the key to Shen Kuo's success.

Wang Mingming:
Shen Kuo

SU SHI

Su Shi (1037-1101), also called Dongpo or Zizhan, was a native of Meishan, Mei Prefecture (present-day Meishan County in Sichuan). He is regarded as one of the greatest poets of the Northern Song Dynasty, and also achieved pre-eminence in painting and calligraphy.

Su Shi enjoyed a very high reputation among the Chinese literati and greatly influenced the history of Chinese literature. He is one of the few Chinese poets whose works convey an attitude of good-humored acceptance.

Educated by his mother, Su Shi had high aspirations in his early youth and passed his imperial examination when he was 20. The court thought highly of him. Loyal to the emperor and to his country, Su Shi studied hard to advance his political career.

However, he was also pessimistic and more world-weary than other writers. Though he never retired from politics, his poetry, articles and paintings became more and more cynical. He admired Tao Yuanming's simple style of writing and peaceful, transcendental mental state.

"Then, suddenly startled, it turns its head,
With a grief that no one can know.
Looking over each wintry bough, it settles on none.
The lonely sandbank's cold."

Driven by a deep loneliness, Su Shi often searched for a fictitious land of peace.

"The bright moon, when will she appear?
Wine cup in hand, I ask the blue sky.
I do not know inside the gates of heaven,
What time it will be tonight."

Su Shi knew he could never be free from his worries, so he studied the writings of Taoist philosophers and acquired a profound knowledge of Buddhism. He was criticized by his contemporaries, "He wants to remain aloof from the world, but he has failed; he tries to divert himself from boredom, but he is mocked by others; he advocates Confucianism, but he believes in Buddhism."

Describing his philosophy, Su Shi wrote,

"I was just about to ride there on the wind,
But feared that heaven's crystalline palaces and towers
So high, would be for me too cold."

Finally, he realized that his attitude must change.

"I looked back, a desolate place where I was from,
Going back, there would be neither storm nor affection."

After changing his philosophical orientation, Su Shi wrote some of his best verses, describing things objectively and displaying his own feelings without prejudice.

With a bold vision, Su Shi controlled his own feelings through his philosophy of life. He vigorously praised life, conveying an attitude of calm, even good-humored acceptance.

With his powerful poetic style, he founded the "unrestrained school" of Song "ci" poetry.

Wang Mingming:
Su Shi

LI QINGZHAO

Li Qingzhao (1084-1155), also called Yi'an Jushi, is renowned in the history of Chinese literature as a graceful, restrained poet of the Song Dynasty.

A woman of the feudal upper class, Li Qingzhao lived happily during the first half of her life. She was a daughter of a distinguished scholar. Gifted and ambitious, she devoted herself to the study of arts in her childhood.

At 18, she was married to Zhao Mingcheng, whose father was a minister. Gentle and educated, her husband was an antiquarian, book collector and writer of witticisms. As artists with the same attitudes towards life, the couple lived happily, pursuing their reading, antiques, painting and calligraphy.

During the Song Dynasty, when the new poetic form "ci" was established, Li Qingzhao won the admiration and respect of many of her contemporaries for her "ci" poetry and for her clear, graceful language. She lived a peaceful life until she was 43 years old, and wrote "ci" to convey her inner thoughts and feelings.

But in 1127 the Jin Army captured Kaifeng and took the Song emperor away. The Northern Song Dynasty was destroyed and the unstable Southern Song Dynasty began. After the death of her husband and the loss of their antique colection, Li Qingzhao drifted from place to place, homeless and miserable. Through her depression, her character matured. Her indignation against the incompetent Song emperors, her deep regret for the lost territory and her hardships gave her poems a new vitality and creativity. As a poet she could be both bold and delicate, languid and boisterous.

"The setting sun melts gold,
  Dusk clouds join walls,
  Where is my man?"

Two kinds of "ci" poetry developed during the Song Dynasty. One is graceful and restrained, and the other is bold and unrestrained. Most of the orthodox poets belonged to the former school, criticizing the latter writers.

In writing, Li Qingzhao used both traditional methods and her own style. Because of the social chaos and her own sober feelings, Li Qingzhao's later works followed the bold and unrestrained school.

Li Qingzhao enjoys a high reputation in Chinese literature, admired by scholars for her fine works and her strong personality

Wang Xijing:
Li Qingzhao

Lu You and Xin Qiji were patriotic writers living after the fall of the Song Dynasty. The closing years of the Song Dynasty saw great political upheavals. The Jin invaded central China, disrupting people's lives. Treacherous court officials in power betrayed their country for their own personal interests, and brought an end to the peaceful life of the Song Dynasty, which had lasted for more than 100 years. Worried, sad and full of hatred, the honest people were eager to fight against the invaders. The whole society was stirred up.

The patriotic idea of fighting against the Jin invaders to recover lost territory replaced literary themes about drink, dance, and affection for close friends and relatives. Noble-minded patriots and scholars, filled with grief and indignation, wrote poems and prose to repudiate the traitors and encourage people to take up arms. The "shi" of Lu You and the "ci" of Xin Qiji, two traditional poetic forms, were good examples of this sincerity and agitation.

LU YOU

Lu You (1125-1210), also called Wuguan, was a native of Shanyin (present-day Shaoxing in Zhejiang Province). When he was young he fled with his father to escape the invading Jin. The experience of being a refugee made a deep impression on him.

Early in his youth, his father taught him how to write poetry, and instilled him with strong patriotic feelings. In his later years, he recalled, "I saw with my own eyes that when scholars and officials were discussing state affairs, some were cursing between their teeth, while others wept bitterly. They pledged to help the emperor and defend the country with their own lives." Their patriotic spirit had a great influence on Lu You.

When he was already past 30, Lu You was appointed a junior official for Fujian and then Lin'an. He never forgot about the territory which had been lost, and wrote two memorials to the emperor to detail his views on politics and military strategy.

He went to Sichuan when he was over 40, gaining military experience on the battlefield. He was deeply moved by the affection of the people in occupied areas for their own country. Worried and depressed, he wrote,

"My clothes are stained with dust and wine,
I have been fascinated with scenes on my trip.
A poet I am,
Riding a donkey to enter the Sword Gate."

In his later years, while holding posts in Jiangxi and Zhejiang, Lu You continued to advocate resistance against the Jin. He finally retired in Shanyin at the age of 66, living a simple life. He was always concerned about the fate of the country and the people. But his hopes of regaining lost territory were never realized.

"I am not sad staying in an isolated village,
Only thinking to defend the border of my country.
Lying in bed on a still night,
I listen to the sounds of rain and wind.
In a dream, I rode a horse to cross a frozen river."

Lu You, renowned for his staunch patriotism and deep feelings, wrote bold and unrestrained poetry, with lush, exotic and allusive language. He is not only admired for his works but for his character and morality.

Wang Mingming:
Lu You

人生不作安期生，醉入東海騎長鯨。猶當出作李西平，手梟逆賊清舊京。金印煌煌未入手，白髮種種來無情。成都古寺臥秋晚，落日偏傍僧窗明。豈其馬上破賊手，哦詩長作寒螿鳴。興來買盡市橋酒，大車磊落堆長瓶。哀絲豪竹助劇飲，如巨野受黃河傾。平時一滴不入口，意氣頓使千人驚。國仇未報壯士老，匣中寶劍夜有聲。何當凱旋宴將士，三更雪壓飛狐城。

放翁詩
歲在癸巳夏
陸放翁造像
石齋

XIN QIJI

Also devoted to the recovery of his homeland, Xin Qiji (1140-1207), sometimes called You'an or Jiaxuan,was a native of Liecheng (now in Shandong). He was born into an official's family. His father died when Xin Qiji was young, and he was brought up by his grandfather Xin Zhan. A man of integrity, Xin Zhan educated his grandson in patriotism by frequently taking him to visit beautiful mountains and rivers.

Xi Qiji grew up a strong man, good both at Chinese and fighting. He showed his talents as a politician and general after he caught and killed several deserters and captured the enemy's generals. Like Lu You, Xin Qiji was dedicated to his country and his people all his life, although he did not fulfil his dream of recovering lost territory.

His masterpiece, *The Poetry of Jiaxuan*, consists of four volumes with more than 600 poems. Xin Qiji's rich experience, extensive imagination and extraordinary talent are reflected in a variety of forms and subjects.

As a poet, Xin Qiji could be both bold and delicate. Some poems are unrestrained like storms and others are gentle like flowers in the spring.

"Turning up the wick, I examine my sword.

I hear a bugle calling me back in my dream."

"In a short time,

Spring comes and goes.

I love spring, but am afraid of flowers which bloom early.

Moreover, there are already countless fallen petals."

He was one of the greatest poets of the Song Dynasty "ci" style.

Like Lu You, Xin Qiji dreamed of reunifying central China. He wrote regretfully, "Sent out to fight, but not winning victory. This often makes heroes drench their clothes with tears."

Wang Mingming:
Xin Qiji

据地一呼吾往矣 万里摇肢动骨

辛弃疾渴望祖国南北共此云分裂之苦他迫切想醒人们必要意记西北神州真诚希望他年妄补天西北都洗喜髭胡膏血但辛弃疾的主张无从实现他仿坐信青山遮不住毕竟东富里行间充满奔腾向前一定要实现祖国统一的战斗精神

癸亥年春于此国少年怀念三辈

明致西石画屋

ZHU XI

Zhu Xi (1130-1200), a native of Wuyuan County, was also called Huian. He was an outstanding philosopher during the Song Dynasty. Together with Zhang Zai and Chen Xian, he founded the *lixue* school.

Lixue is an idealist Confucian philosophy, combining the doctrines of Buddhism and Taoism. Using the rational spirit of the Confucian school, the theory tried to rationalize feudal society. Ever since Confucius, Chinese philosophers had been trying to unify the people, rationalize the feudal system and formalize the culture and psychology of China. *Lixue* succeeded.

Unification under the Qin and Han dynasties formed the Han nationality. This unification had been rationalized theoretically by Dong Zhongshu, who presented a philosophical system covering nature, society and human beings. After the Han Dynasty, China suffered from factionalism which lasted until the Tang Dynasty. People of the unified Tang Dynasty called themselves "Tang people." In the subsequent unified Song Dynasty, *lixue* emerged.

Like the philosophy of Dong Zhongshu, this philosophy appeared to be a return to the past. But it was actually a complete and rich school of thought. The two major concepts of the *lixue* are "li" and "qi", which are inseparable. Zhu Xi stressed that human desire is antagonistic to "tian-li", or heavenly reason. He asked people to subject their individual desire to heavenly reason.

Lixue was soon adopted by the emperor, and became a major theoretical guide for ruling people. When China was dominated by non-Han peoples during the Yuan and Qing dynasties, these rulers also followed *lixue*.

Born into a declined landlord family, Zhu Xi read widely and believed in Confucianism. He passed the highest imperial examination at 19, and was an official until he died at the age of 70. During his lifetime, he spent more than 40 years theorizing and writing. He annotated and improved many classics.

Annotations of the Analects of Confucius and *Annotations of Mencius*, representative works of *lixue*, formally recorded Zhu Xi's theory. But the scholar offended Emperor Xiaozong and his theory was banned. Nine years after the emperor's death, the court came to understand the real value of *lixue* and issued an imperial edict to mourn Zhu Xi and soothe his family. Zhu Xi's two classic works were listed as official court textbooks, and *lixue* was firmly established.

Wang Mingming:
Zhu Xi

WEN TIANXIANG

A great national hero, a statesman and a patriotic poet during the late Southern Song Dynasty, Wen Tianxiang (1236-1282), also called Lushan, or Wenshan, was a native of Luling (present-day Ji'an of Jiangxi Province).

While Wen Tianxiang was utterly loyal, patriotic and steadfast in the war of resistance against the Mongol invaders, the Southern Song court he served was corrupt and content with temporary ease and comfort.

At the time when Wen Tianxiang was assigned an official post in the capital after winning the title of "No.1 scholar" from the highest imperial examination, the Mongolian rulers north of the Great Wall were preparing an invasion. Having overwhelmed first the Xia and the Jin, the Mongols were advancing south in a three-pronged column.

Not long after he arrived in the capital, Wen Tianxiang suggested to the emperor that the Song armies meet the approaching enemies head-on with a divided force and that Dong Songchen, a eunuch and the leader of the capitulationist clique in the court, be executed to boost the nation's morale. The bold suggestions offended many in the court. Wen Tianxiang was forced to abandon his official post and leave the capital for his hometown.

In the first moon of 1275, news came that the Yuan army — the Mongolian troops — was crossing the Changjiang River. The Southern Song Dynasty was in imminent danger. The desperate Emperor Gongdi issued an imperial edict summoning all people for emergency service. Wen Tianxiang immediately answered the edict and organized a disciplined army 10,000 strong in Gangzhou (present-day Ji'an of Jiangxi Province). Soon he was promoted to the post of "Youchengxiang," or premier.

However, the decline of the Southern Song Dynasty was irreversible. Wen Tianxiang and his men, after repeated battles, retreated on December 11, 1278, to Haifeng (in present-day Guandong Province) and were surprised by the Yuan army. Wen Tianxiang was taken captive and attempted suicide by taking poison but failed.

In February 1279, Yashan (present-day Xinhui County of Guandong Province) fell to the Yuan army and the last Southern Song emperor, Bing, drowned himself in the sea, ending the Southern Song Dynasty.

Wen Tianxiang went on a hunger strike in protest on the way to Dadu (Beijing) under escort — he said he would rather die than submit. Kublai Khan, the first emperor of the Yuan Dynasty, however, kept him alive in prison, attempting to lure him into surrender in hopes of winning popular support. Four years passed and Wen Tianxiang remained firm in purpose. In confinement he wrote the splendid poem *The Song of Righteousness*, which includes the two inspiring lines:

"Death befalls all men alike and I choose to die,
So that my loyal heart will shine in the history of humanity."

In 1282 Wen Tianxiang finally died. People have always celebrated this national hero.

Wang Xijing:
Wen Tianxiang

HUANG DAOPO

Known as Granny Huang, Huang Daopo (1245-?) was born in the last years of the Southern Song Dynasty in Wunijing in Songjiang Prefecture (present-day Shanghai County).

Huang Daopo was highly skilled in spinning and weaving. Very little was recorded about her in history. She was sold to a family as a child bride at the age of 12 or 13. She worked hard and was frequently beaten by her in-laws. One day they locked her in a small woodshed, and she escaped by making a hole in the roof. She hid herself in a boat on the Huangpu River, which took her all the way to Yazhou (in present-day Guangdong), a unique land inhabited by Miao minority people.

She lived in Yazhou for two or three decades, and didn't return to her hometown until she was grey at the temples. Back home, she eventually developed a new process of spinning and weaving called "rolling, fluffing, spinning and weaving." She improved the then advanced textile technology she brought with her from Yazhou and refined the spinning and weaving equipment and tools of her hometown.

In ancient China, silk and hemp fabrics dominated. While silk and hemp texile technology can be traced back more than 2,000 years, the cotton textile industry developed comparatively late.

According to historical records, in the Han Dynasty (206 B.C.-220 A.D.) cotton already grew abundantly in China's southwest and northwest. Yet it was not until the Song Dynasty that cotton spinning and weaving, with very primitive tools, first began in the Changjiang River Valley. Light and soft, and a very good thermal insulation material, cotton's economic value and pupularity grew. Cotton fabrics gradually superseded hemp cloth, and silk also declined since it was troublesome to raise silkworms and grow mulberry trees.

Huang Daopo greatly advanced cotton textile technology, and her hometown in Songjiang was once the center of the cotton textile industry. At the time, the cloth produced in Songjiang was renowned as "the best under heaven."

Although feudal historians ignored the contributions made by working women like Huang Daopo, the common people have always remembered her in folk rhymes.

"Granny Huang, O, Granny Huang,
Teaches me how to weave,
Teaches me how to spin.
I get two bolts of cloth,
With the yarn from two bobbins."

Wang Xijing:
Huang Daopo

LI SHIZHEN

The great Ming Dynasty medical scientist, Li Shizhen (1518-1593) was also known as Dongbi, or Binhu. He was born in Qizhou (present-day Qichuan County in Hubei Province).

Chinese medicine is a treasure house with a history of several thousand years. According to an ancient legend, Shen Nong, the earliest king of China, tasted hundreds of medicinal herbs to test their curative effects. Because of this, China's pioneer pharmacological work, published in the Han Dynasty (206 BC-220 AD), was called *Shen Nong's Canon on Meteria Medica*. During the fifth to sixth century, Tao Hongjing of the Liang Dynasty published *Notes to Materia Medica*, describing new medicines. In 659, the Imperial Medical Academy of the Tang Dynasty published *Revised Materia Medica*, the first complete medical book in the world, containing notes on 844 medicines. The great pharmacologist Li Shizhen of the Ming Dynasty incorporated the strong points of all these medical works to compile his *Compendium of Materia Medica*.

Li Shizhen was born in the countryside with mountains and rivers rich in medicinal herbs. Li always followed his parents to collect herbs in the mountains when he was a young boy and learned to identify various herbs. He also helped his father treat the villagers.

Li Shizhen realized through long years of medical service the importance of correct identification and appropriate application of medicines. But he found that the available books on pharmacology were incomplete and sometimes incorrect. Determined to compile a new book, Li Shizhen collected many recipes from among the masses and extensively read medical works. At the same time, he corrected and expanded the material. For instance, in order to know the medical use of a kind of snake called Huqi, he climbed mountains and crossed rivers to catch it. He went to the sea to ask fishermen about fish breeding. He went deep into mountains and forests to catch animals and study their habits and characteristics. He even risked being poisoned to taste and appraise the medicinal value of various plants, seeds and fruits.

Li Shizhen completed his *Compendium of Materia Medica* after travelling through more than half of China and surmounting untold hardships and difficulties. His research took more than 20 years. *Compendium of Materia Medica* was issued in 50 volumes, amounting to 1.9 million words. It lists 1,892 medicines and 11,091 recipes and prescriptions. No ancient pharmaceutical work in Chinese history can equal this monumental treatise.

Li Shizhen died in 1593. But the contribution he made is immortal. His work first appeared in 1596 and was all the rage of the time. It was introduced to Japan in 1606. Later, it was translated into Latin, French, Russian, German and English. It is now part of the world's treasure of medical science.

Wang Xijing:
Li Shizhen

GUAN HANQING

Guan Hanqing (?), a Yuan Dynasty dramatist, was a native of Dadu (Beijing). A keen playwright, he worked for a long time in opera houses and theatres and later became a representative of the "zaju" school.

"Zaju", poetic drama set to music, flourished during the Yuan Dynasty. It is the source of China's dramatic art. Dramatic literature, like Tang poetry and Song "ci" (a kind of verse), bears the distinctive mark of its time. In the Mongol-ruled Yuan Dynasty, the Confucian school was on the decline and the long-established ethics and theories of the past no longer played a guiding role in the literary world.

The court attached little importance to the "Four Books" and the "Five Classics"* and hardly valued well-read scholars. The abolition of the imperial examination system drew interest away from classical poems and stereotyped writings and from the doctrines of Confucius and Mencius. Under these conditions "zaju" began to take shape.

Incorporating music, dance-acting, dialogue and make-up, "zaju" originated from an artistic psychology of imitation. Later, role-playing developed to either present a long story or to create several clear-cut images within a limited time.

Guan Hanqing was good at role-playing. From his make-up alone, the audience could tell the character's social standing and background, and the facial make-up helped the character speak his mind easily and freely. Familiar with the artistic idea of role-playing, Guan Hanqing made full use of it in his "zaju" to unfold the plot and push it quickly to a climax.

"Zaju" was extremely popular with the city people. Guan Hanqing knew their life and their psychology, and offered plays which appealed to them directly. Yet his drama also possesses that prominent feature of any great art — it illuminates the journey of complex individuals.

Guan Hanqing was quick, witty and tenacious. In one of his rhymes entitled *Not Yielding to Old Age*, he likened himself to a brass pea which could not be steamed soft, hammered flat or fried to burst.

He wrote more than 60 plays, which have had a great impact on Chinese drama. His popularity and influence can be compared to that of Shakespeare.

*"Four Books" refers to *The Great Learning*, *The Doctrine of the Mean*, *The Analects of Confucius* and *Mencius*. "Five Classics" refers to *The Book of Songs*, *The Book of History*, *the Book of Changes*, *The Book of Rites* and *The Spring and Autumn Annals*. Both the "Four Books" and the "Five Classics" are the quintessence of China's feudal ethics and teachings.

Wang Mingming:
Guan Hanqing

PU SONGLING

Called the Lay Buddhist of Liuquan (Willow Spring), Pu Songling (1640-1715) was a native of Shandong Province and a noted novelist of the Qing Dynasty. He wrote *Tales of Liaozhai*, a group of stories which established his reputation as a literary eccentric.

Although *Tales of Liaozhai* is about ghosts and spirits, the stories are moving and romantic rather than scary. Pu Songling tried to describe the beautiful things on earth by connecting them with the supernatural.

In one story, a fox spirit who has become a beautiful woman falls in love with a man and marries him. To his surprise, her love and tenderness far surpass the traditional love between husband and wife which, according to feudal ethics, was supposed to be as between guest and host.

But the girl's in-laws will not accept her, and she is forced to leave. As she goes, she reveals to her husband that she is not human, but a fox spirit. The shocking disclosure, however, does not shake his firm love for her, and he simply wants to go with her. Unfortunately, as a human he cannot.

Pu Songling loved the unrestrained and beautiful in life, and felt weighed down by the rigidly stratified feudal society. He created a fantasy world of ghosts and spirits in which he could escape to the true, the good and the beautiful.

Brilliant and cultured as he was, Pu Songling was very poor and consequently had to study stereotyped classical writing in preparation for the imperial examination. He worked long years for an official position through the exams, but it was not until he was 71 years old that he acquired a petty academic degree.

Pu Songling was born in the late Ming Dynasty and matured in the early Qing Dynasty, when fiction dominated Chinese literature. His work is regarded as exemplary of the times, and still enjoys great popularity.

Wang Xijing:
Pu Songling

ZHENG BANQIAO

Zheng Banqiao (1693-1765) called himself Kerou. He was a painter and scholar during the Qing Dynasty.

Zheng was born into a scholar's family in Xinghua, in present-day Jiangsu Province. Although his family was originally somewhat wealthy, it had declined by Zheng Banqiqo's time.His mother died early and he was brought up by a village woman named Fei.

When he was 30 years old, Zheng's father and wife both died. This tragedy, plus his failure in the imperial examinations, caused a mental breakdown. He wandered around in a romantic dream, which he described this way:

"Begging food from a mountain temple,
Having clothes mended at a singing girl's home."

In the first years of the reign of Emperor Qianlong, 44-year-old Zheng Banqiao won success in the highest imperial examination. He was made a county magistrate in what is now Shandong Province, and stayed there until he was 61.

Zheng Banqiao was sympathetic to people. In the 11th and 12th year of the emperor's reign, his county was hit by a famine so serious that the starving people began eating each other. Zheng Banqiao ordered the granary to be opened to prevent more deaths. When the fall came and no harvest was forthcoming, he publicly burned all the debtors' notes. The people were so grateful they erected a temple in his honor. However, his jealous superior demoted Zheng.

Back in Yangzhou, Zheng Banqiao remained in high spirits. He continued to live by selling his paintings of cymbidiums, bamboos and rocks. His paintings are precise and neat, and feature craggy rocks which reflect his unbending spirit. His bamboos are powerful, yet have tender leaves. They show the beauty of strength.

Zheng Banqiao was also a humorous man. He liked to scratch a few amusing lines on his paintings. Very often he was in high spirits after he had finished a painting and excitedly talked about the ideas contained in the work.

He also wrote down exactly what was in his mind. Many of his theories have been preserved, such as "ideas come before art."

Wang Mingming:
Zheng Banqiao

CAO XUEQIN

A literary giant of the Qing Dynasty, Cao Xueqin (1715-1763) was also called Qinpu, or Qinxi. His masterpiece belongs not only to China but also to the whole world.

The Qing Dynasty (1644-1911) was the last feudal dynasty in China, and *A Dream of Red Mansions* by Cao Xueqin was the last brilliant literary work ever produced in feudal society. The novel appeared under Emperor Qianlong (the mid-18th century).

Cao Xueqin was born into a noble Manchu family which "had been illustrious for nearly a hundred years," next only to the royal family. The family owned splendid estates with tastefully furnished houses and exquisite gardens. They indulged in pleasure and ease, glittering wealth and wanton luxury, collected fine works of art, and affected manners as well. But before long all this was lost, and Cao Xueqin, in his late years, lived in poverty and misery.

Under these unfortunate circumstances, he began to write *A Dream of Red Mansions*. The book artistically depicts the fabulous wealth and declining grandeur of Chinese feudal society and predicts its inevitable doom. The author sought a retreat in his writing from his loneliness and his regret over the past.

Nurtured culturally and intellectually by his family and abundantly furnished with material from life for his novel, Cao Xueqin became keenly aware of his surroundings, his country's past and its future. The characters are described in detail and presented as part of their social milieu, conveying the pulse of the historical period.

There are several hundred characters, all clearly and realistically portrayed. Among them, Jia Baoyu and Lin Daiyu stand out. Their sentimental dispositions, bright minds, beautiful looks, pure passion and tragic love greatly appeal to the readers.

A Dream of Red Mansions has developed a reputation as "an encyclopedia of Chinese feudal society" and research on the book is a specific academic pursuit in present-day China.

Wang Mingming:
Cao Xueqin

About the Painters

Wang Xijing was born in Xi'an in 1946. As a child, he hungrily read books on history, literature and painting, compiling 70,000 characters of notes.

At 15, Wang Xijing was admitted to the middle school affiliated with the Xi'an Academy of Fine Arts, where his talent developed. He diligently studied and practised drawing. On Sundays and during the summer and winter vacations, he often hiked dozens of kilometres to paint and gather ideas in out-of-the-way places.

The "cultural revolution" (1966-76) prevented Wang Xijing from entering college, but he studied on his own. Fascinated by painting and its theory, he surprised people by finishing a draft of a 140,000-character book, *A Study of Line Drawing of Chinese Figure Painting*. In the meantime, his artistic style matured.

In 1979 he became a fine arts editor for the *Xi'an Daily* There he devoted himself to drawing and research , and published a book on fine brushwork and figure painting techniques.

Wang Xijing is a prolific painter, with more than 1,000 works appearing in various publications. Some of his works won local and national prizes. His paintings are natural and accessible. His portraits of historical figures were praised by masters for their firm brushstrokes and flowing lines.

Wang Xijing strives to be a well-rounded artist by studying literature, poetry, music, dance, drama and folk arts.

He was elected a council member of the Shaanxi branch of the Chinese Artists Association in 1980 and two years later was invited to be fine arts advisor to the Shaanxi Teachers College. He is currently Vice-Chairman of the Xi'an Artists Association.

Wang Mingming was born into an intellectual's family in Beijing in 1952. He began to draw when he was a child, under his father's guidance. He attended the Beijing Children's Palace when he was 8 to 14 years old. During this period he frequently won national and international children's painting contests. His works were exhibited in a dozen countries.

Unfortunately, the "cultural revolution" (1966-76) interrupted Wang Mingming's studies. He worked in a factory while he continued to study by himself, collecting ideas for subjects and visiting masters. After more than 10 years, Wang Mingming's art flourished. In 1978, he joined the staff at the Beijing Academy of Fine Arts. He had the opportunity to study art theory, learn from master painters and paint outside Beijing.

Wang Mingming innovates in traditional Chinese painting. "Living in a modern society, we should have a fresh understanding of historical material," Wang Mingming said.

Wang Mingming combines Western painting techniques with traditional Chinese art. His paintings of historical figures depict ancient people in a modern style. His recent works were welcomed in Japan, France, Singapore, Canada and Hongkong.

Wang Mingming also studies oil painting, engraving and pottery, to bring new dimensions to his art.

CATALOGUE

书名题字：蒋兆和
封面图：林　墉

中国著名历史人物画传
（英文版）

王西京　王明明　绘画
马　悦　王燕荣　编著
出版者：朝　华　出　版　社
（中国国际图书贸易总公司出版机构）
中国北京车公庄西路21号
印刷者：上海市印刷一厂
中国上海齐齐哈尔路920号
发行者：中国国际图书贸易总公司
（中国国际书店）
中国北京第399号信箱
1989年第一版
02000（英）　84E－638P
ISBN 7-5054-0095-9/K.0038